MY SYSTEM of CAREER INFLUENCES
MSCI (Adolescent)

A Qualitative Career Assessment
Reflection Process

Workbook

(Second Edition)

MARY MCMAHON, WENDY PATTON, MARK WATSON

www.
AUSTRALIANACADEMIC**PRESS**
.com.au

First published in 2017
Australian Academic Press Group Pty. Ltd.
18 Victor Russell Drive,
Samford QLD 4520, Australia
www.australianacademicpress.com.au

ISBN 9781922117809

Publisher: Stephen May

Cover design and typesetting: Maria Biaggini

Printing: Lightning Source

Contents

About the Authors

Mary McMahon

Dr Mary McMahon is an Honorary Senior Lecturer in the School of Education at The University of Queensland, Australia. Her particular interests are the career development of children and adolescents, and the application of constructivist approaches to career counselling and assessment. She is especially interested in qualitative career assessment. Mary is the author of a number of books, book chapters, and refereed journal articles.

Wendy Patton

Professor Wendy Patton is Emeritus Professor in the Faculty of Education at Queensland University of Technology, Australia. She has published extensively in the area of career development, including articles, book chapters, conference papers, and a number of co-authored and co-edited books. She is currently on the editorial advisory boards of a number of national and international career development journals and the Series Editor of the *Career Development Series* with Sense Publishers.

Mark Watson

Mark Watson is a Distinguished Professor of Psychology at the Nelson Mandela Metropolitan University, South Africa. He specialises in career, school and adolescent psychology and researches lifespan career development, with a specific focus on assessment and cross-cultural issues. He publishes in international and national journals, is the author of book chapters and is co-editor of several books. He is currently on the editorial advisory boards of several international career development journals.

Introduction

Career decision making can be both exciting and challenging. Throughout your life you will make many career decisions and transitions. Each decision may be subject to a range of influences, for example people you know may give an opinion, you may be attracted to work in a particular place or with a particular salary, the organisation you work for may restructure, or you may simply want a change. It is useful to think about these influences and their impact on you.

The My System of Career Influences (Adolescent) will provide you with an opportunity to reflect on or think about the influences on your career decision. It will guide you through a step by step reflection process.

The MSCI (Adolescent) has been used successfully by many young people who have found it a useful way to look holistically at, and to begin conversations with people such as parents and teachers, about their career decisions. We hope that you will also find the experience of completing the MSCI (Adolescent) beneficial in your career decision making.

Reflecting on my career decisions

During adolescence you may make the first of many career decisions that you will make during your life. For example, you may make decisions about choosing subjects and what you are going to do when you leave school. Some adolescents find career decision making complex and confusing. One reason for this can be all of the factors that influence your career decision making. For example, people such as your family, teachers and friends may offer support and advice and you may need to think about factors such as financial costs and future employment prospects. Making sense of such an array of varied influences can be challenging.

Completing this booklet will help you think about the many factors that may influence your career decisions. There are usually many influences that adolescents have to consider before they can make career decisions. Your parents, your current school, your grades in school, your friends, where you live and your lifestyle dreams influence the present thoughts you have about your career direction. Influences such as these can direct you toward or away from a choice, and are not necessarily positive or negative.

Most people find that identifying their own influences helps them to understand what is important to them in their career decisions.

As you work through this booklet, read the instructions carefully and take your time. This will help you to identify the most important influences for you in relation to your career decision making at this time.

It is important to be aware that you will make many career decisions throughout your life, and that these influences and their level of importance to you will vary over time. Even during your teenage years, you will make a number of career decisions. For that reason, we encourage you to complete this reflection process more than once.

Name: ....

Date of first completion: ....

Date of second completion: ....

Notes

This page provides a space for you to make notes about the career decision you are currently making, for example, is there a timeframe, what is exciting you or worrying you about your decision making.

My present career situation

In the spaces provided, answer the following questions to start thinking about your life and the career decision you have to make.

1. What career decisions do you need to make in the future? For example, you may need to choose subjects at school, or you may be thinking about your first part-time job or what you will do when you leave school.

   ....

   ....

   ....

2. List below any part-time or volunteer work you have considered or have done at any time in the past or you are doing at present.

   ....

   ....

   ....

3. Think about life-roles you have other than that of student. These may include roles such as sportsperson, choir member, class captain, youth group member.

   ....

   ....

   ....

4. List below any careers that you have considered for your future.

   ....

   ....

   ....

5. List below any previous career decisions that you have made (e.g., choosing subjects to study, choosing to continue or discontinue activities such as music or sport).

   ....

   ....

   ....

6. What strategies or approaches have you used in your previous decision-making?

   ....

   ....

   ....

7. Who has helped you or provided advice with your previous career decisions?

....

....

....

Notes

In the space below, make notes about anything else that you think could be relevant to your career decision making.

Thinking about who I am

When people are making career decisions there are usually many influences that make them unique. For example, you may have an outgoing personality, or a special ability such as being good at mathematics. It may be important to you to earn a lot of money or to help people.

On the diagram below are some examples of influences on career decisions. Read the examples carefully and take time to think about yourself.

1. Tick the influences that may apply to your next career decision and make notes related to these influences if this is useful to you.

2. Write on the diagram any other influences you can think of that are not listed.

3. Mark with an asterisk (*) those that you think are really important or a big influence on you.

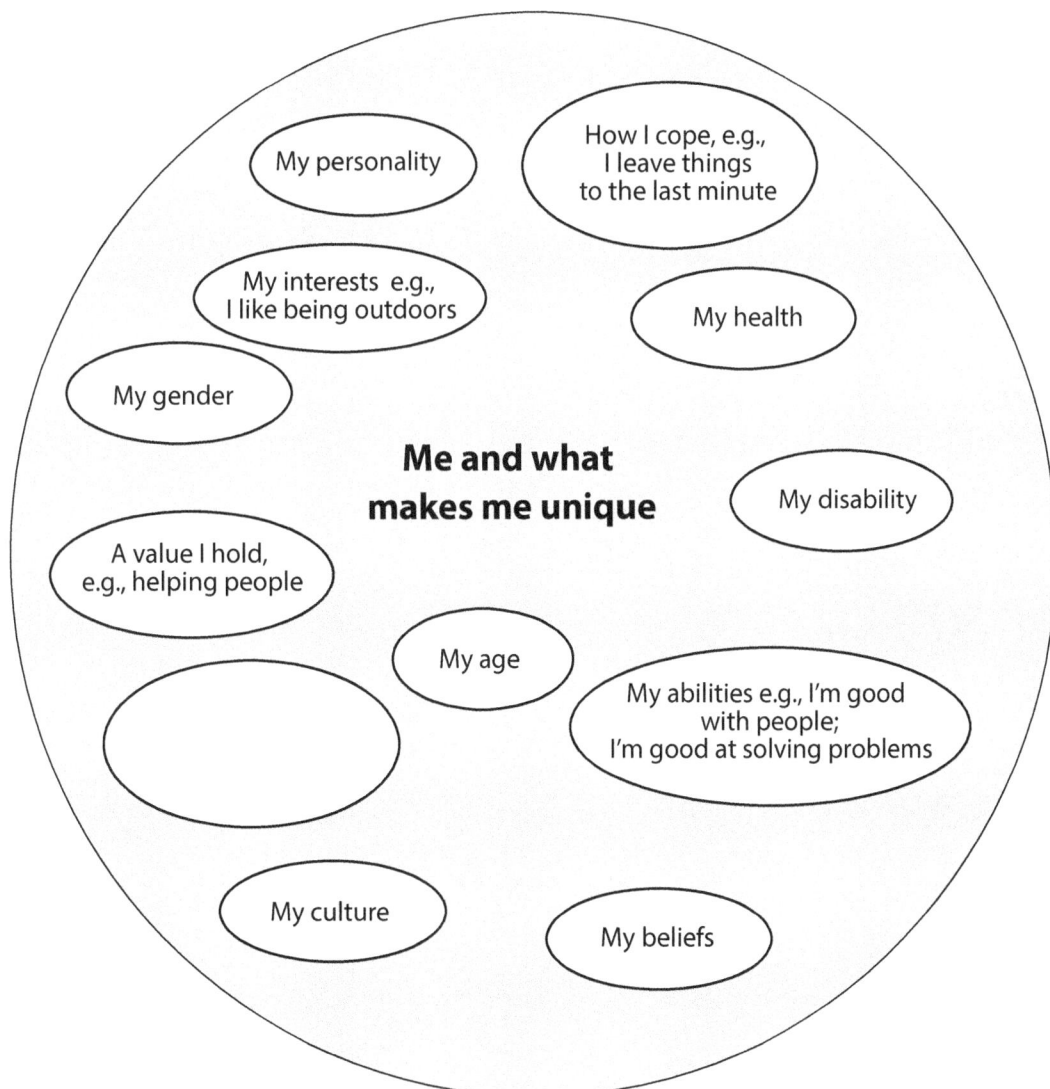

Notes

MY SYSTEM OF CAREER INFLUENCES: Adolescent Workbook

Thinking about the people around me

When people make career decisions, sometimes others around them may influence their thinking. For example, parents may suggest careers they think are suitable, you may have talked to someone whose career sounds interesting, or someone, e.g. a sister, brother, or friend may be critical of something you want to do. Sometimes people read about or see or hear something on TV or radio that influences their decision.

On the diagram below are some examples of influences on career decisions. Read them carefully and take time to think about your own life.

1. Tick the influences that apply to your next career decision and make notes related to these influences if this is useful to you.

2. Add any others that you can think of that are not listed.

3. Mark with an asterisk (*) those that you think are really important or are a big influence on you.

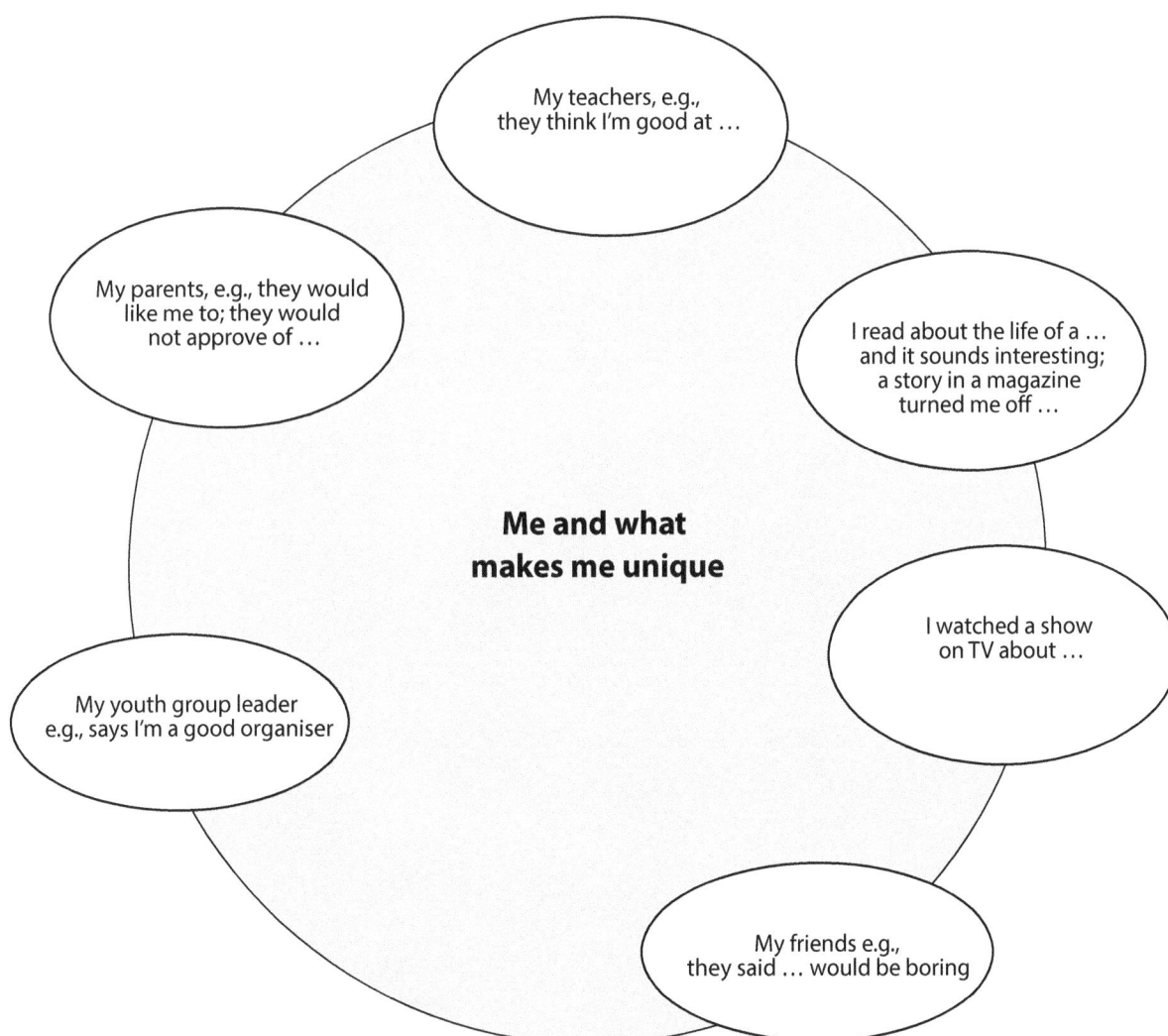

My teachers, e.g., they think I'm good at …

My parents, e.g., they would like me to; they would not approve of …

I read about the life of a … and it sounds interesting; a story in a magazine turned me off …

Me and what makes me unique

I watched a show on TV about …

My youth group leader e.g., says I'm a good organiser

My friends e.g., they said … would be boring

Notes

MY SYSTEM OF CAREER INFLUENCES: Adolescent Workbook

Thinking about society and the environment

When people are making career decisions, it is sometimes important to consider the influence of the society in which they live and the environment around them. For example, some people live in areas where there are few career opportunities, and for others the cost of a study course or living expenses, or the availability of transport may influence their decision.

On the diagram below are some examples of influences on career decisions. Read the examples carefully and take time to think about your own life.

1. Tick the influences that apply to your next career decision and make notes related to these influences if this is useful to you.

2. Add any others that you can think of that are not listed.

3. Mark with an asterisk (*) those that you think are really important or are a big influence on you.

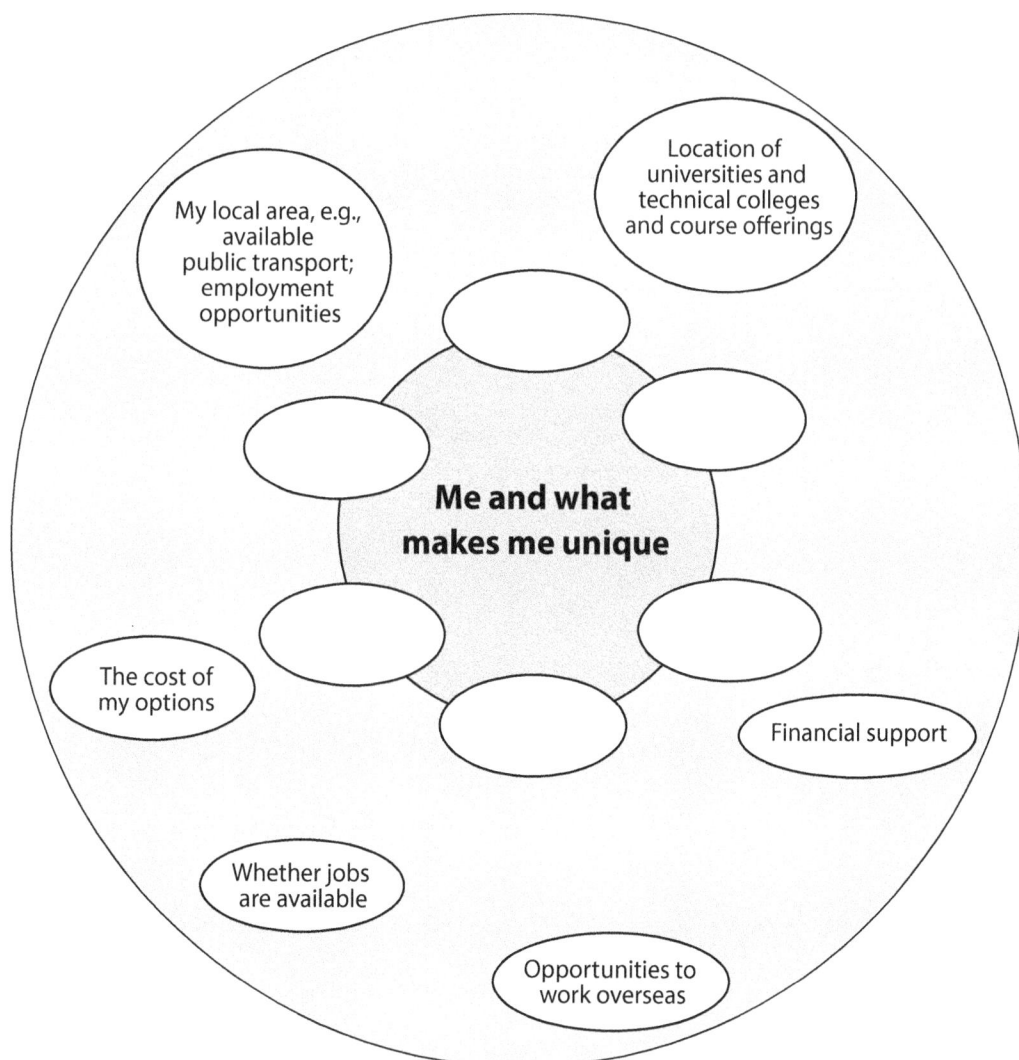

Notes

MY SYSTEM OF CAREER INFLUENCES: Adolescent Workbook

Thinking about my past, present and future

Some of the influences you have already considered may have occurred in the past and yet still affect your career decision. For example, you may have seen a movie years ago that gave you some ideas about a career that interests you.

Sometimes decisions may be influenced by future considerations. For example, some people may know that they want to work overseas.

Sometimes career decisions may be affected by things in people's present lives that they want to keep the same or want to change. For example, they may not want to move from where they currently live.

On the diagram below are some examples of influences on career decisions. Read the examples carefully and take time to think about your own life.

1. Tick the influences that apply to your next career decision and make notes related to these influences if this is useful to you.

2. Add any others that you can think of that are not listed.

3. Mark with an asterisk (*) those that you think are really important or are a big influence on you.

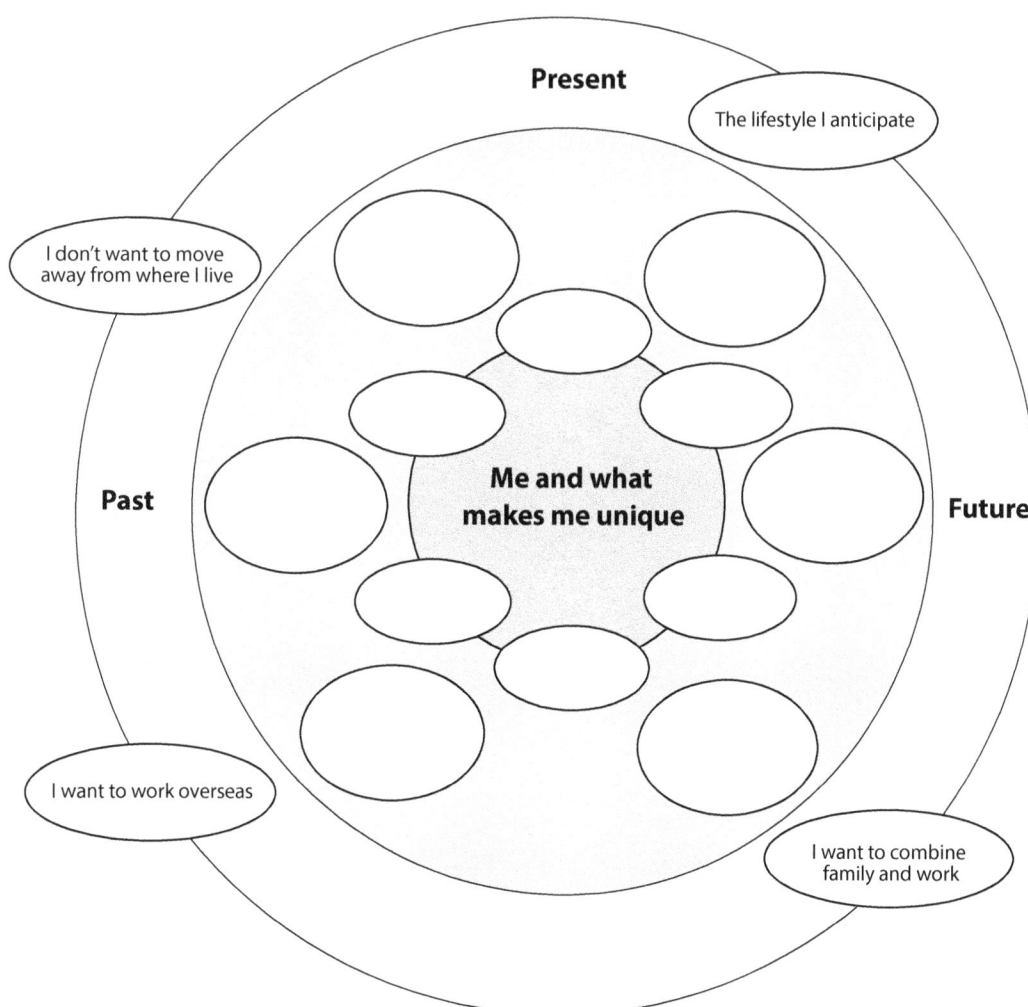

Present

The lifestyle I anticipate

I don't want to move away from where I live

Past

Me and what makes me unique

Future

I want to work overseas

I want to combine family and work

Notes

Representing My System of Career Influences

Now that you have had a chance to reflect on some influences on your career decision, it is time for you to put them all together in one diagram on page 17 of this booklet. Below is an example that may help you.

Work in pencil so that you can erase easily. You will need to turn back through the pages you have just completed. You will notice that the diagrams you have already completed on pages 7– 13 build on each other to provide a comprehensive picture of your System of Career Influences.

Follow these step-by-step instructions to represent your System of Career Influences in one diagram on page 17.

1. Turn back to Page 7.

First of all, think about where you want to place yourself in the diagram. Are you in the centre, off to one side, or in a corner? How will you represent yourself, e.g., as a circle, a square, or some other shape? How big will you be? How will you represent the other influences you identified on this page? Think about how big these influences are? Where will they be in relation to you?

2. Go to Pages 9, 11, and 13 in turn.

Think about where you will place each influence on your diagram. As you place each influence on your diagram, think about its size and shape. How large or small will it be? How close to or far away from you will it be? What shape will it be? What will be adjacent to it or overlapping it?

3. Once you have finished your diagram, you may use colours, symbols or pictures to complete your diagram.

4. You have now completed a diagram of your System of Career Influences.

Example: Jane's System of Career Influences

Jane is fifteen years old and chose to represent her System of Career Influences in this way. She has included influences from each page of the workbook. You can see that Jane had two influences from Page 7 to include in her system, two influences from Page 9, two from Page 11, and one from Page 13.

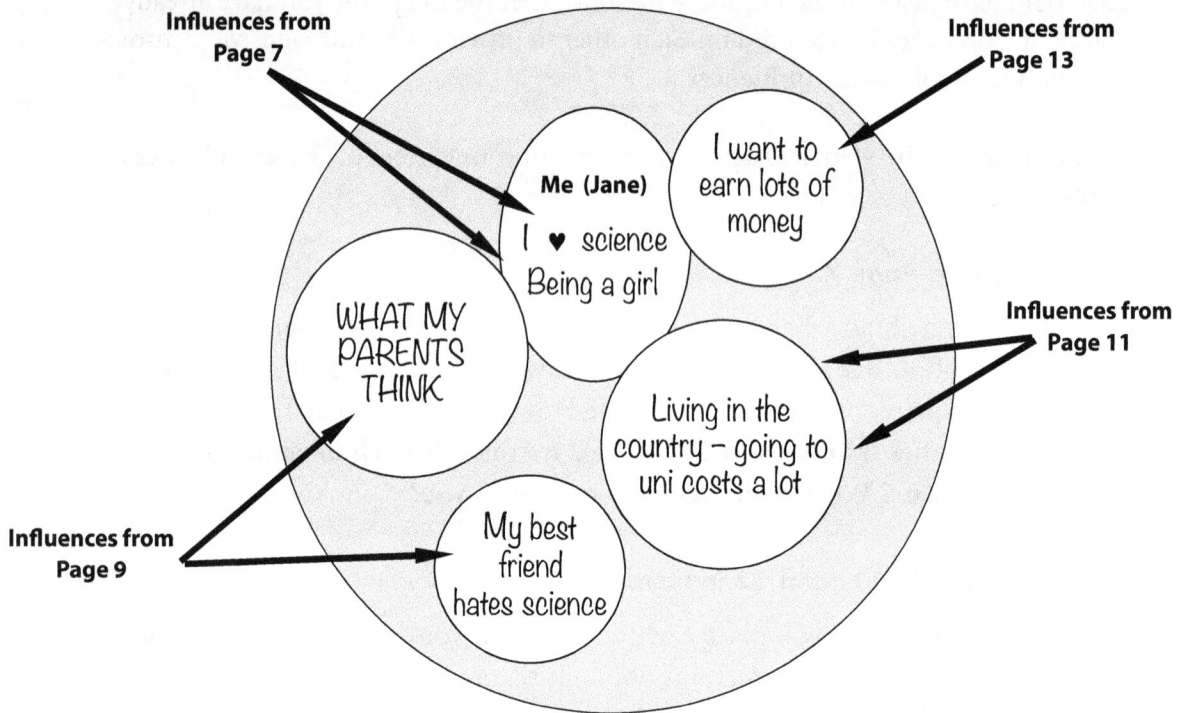

Influences from Page 7

Influences from Page 13

Influences from Page 11

Influences from Page 9

Me (Jane)
I ♥ science
Being a girl

I want to earn lots of money

WHAT MY PARENTS THINK

Living in the country – going to uni costs a lot

My best friend hates science

Notes

My System of Career Influences

Date of completion: ....

Notes

MY SYSTEM OF CAREER INFLUENCES: Adolescent Workbook

Reflecting on My System of Career Influences

Now that you have drawn your System of Career Influences, it is time to reflect on what you have noticed or become aware of. The following questions might guide your thinking as you look at your diagram.

- What influences are most important for you?

  ....

  ....

- What influences are least important for you?

  ....

  ....

- What has surprised you about your System of Career Influences?

  ....

  ....

- What have you noticed that you were not previously aware of?

  ....

  ....

- What has been confirmed for you?

  ....

  ....

- What would you like to change?

  ....

  ....

- What would you like to remain the same?

  ....

  ....

- How do you feel as you look at your System of Career Influences?

  ....

  ....

- Of those influences you located closest to you, which do you think is most important? How do you explain its importance?

  ....

  ....

- Which of these influences have you encountered in previous career decisions? How did they help you? If they did not help you, how did you deal with them?

  ....

  ....

Notes

My action plan

Now that you have completed your MSCI diagram and reflected on its meaning to you and the story it tells, it is time to think about what you might do next in your career decision making process. These questions will help you to plan your next steps.

• Who will you talk to about your System of Career Influences diagram and what would you like to tell them?

  ....

  ....

• What action or steps will you take now that you have completed your Systems of Career Influences diagram?

  ....

  ....

• What information would you like to find out now?

  ....

  ....

• Who could you speak to for that information?

  ....

  ....

• What resources could you use to find out more?

  ....

  ....

Notes

My System of Career Influences II

Date of completion: ....

This page provides a space where you can construct another System of Career Influences diagram some time after you complete your first diagram. Prior to doing this, work through the booklet again taking care to distinguish your previous answers from your new answers.

Learning about my career development

- What differences and similarities have you noticed between your present System of Career Influences II and the System you constructed previously?

    ....

    ....

- How do you explain those differences and similarities?

    ....

    ....

My Action Plan

- Who will you talk to about your System of Career Influences II diagram and what would you like to tell them?

    ....

    ....

- What action or steps will you take now that you have completed your Systems of Career Influences II diagram?

    ....

    ....

- What information would you like to find out now?

    ....

    ....

- Who could you speak to for that information?

    ....

    ....

- What resources could you use to find out more?

    ....

    ....